SCIENCE
GETS IT
WRONG

LET'S MAKE
SOME
GOLD!

SCIENCE'S BIGGEST
MISTAKES ABOUT
GEOLOGY AND ECOLOGY

CHRISTINE ZUCHORA-WALSKE

Lerner Publications Company • Minneapolis

Lerner Publications Company
A division of Lerner Publishing Group, Inc.
241 First Avenue North
Minneapolis, MN 55401 USA

For reading levels and more information, look up this title at www.lernerbooks.com.

Main body text set in Avenir LT Pro Regular 12/18.
Typeface provided by Linotype AG.

Library of Congress Cataloging-in-Publication Data

Zuchora-Walske, Christine.
     Let's make some gold! : science's biggest mistakes about geology and ecology / by Christine Zuchora-Walske.
       pages cm. — (Science gets it wrong)
     Includes index.
     ISBN 978–1–4677–3662–6 (lib. bdg. : alk. paper)
     ISBN 978–1–4677–4736–3 (eBook)
     1. Errors, Scientific—Juvenile literature. 2. Science—History—Popular works—Juvenile literature. I. Title.
     Q172.5.E77Z83 2015
     001.9'6—dc23   2013050849

Manufactured in the United States of America
1 — DP — 7/15/14

CONTENTS

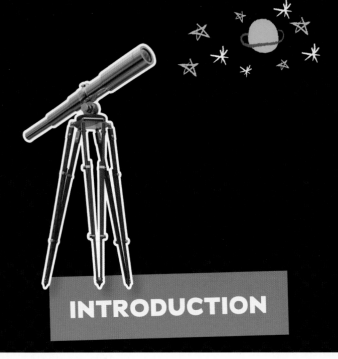

Earth is flat. California is an island. You can mix other metals to make gold.

In earlier times, many people believed ideas like these. They were once examples of the best available scientific thinking.

For as long as humans have existed, we've tried to understand our surroundings. For centuries, people used simple methods to examine Earth. They tried to figure out the rules that nature follows. They asked questions, made observations, and performed tests. These steps became the basis of science. Over time, people developed new scientific tools. In the 1800s, scientists began digging deep underground and learning more about the structure of the planet.

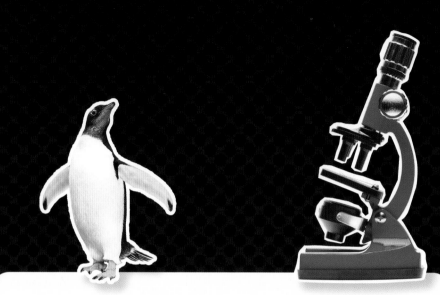

As we humans improved our scientific knowledge, sometimes we confirmed old ideas about Earth. Sometimes we realized we'd been terribly wrong. Oops!

Science is a constant search for new facts. And new facts can reveal problems with old ideas.

So go ahead and laugh at the silly science of the past. But remember: someday people might think our scientific ideas are pretty goofy too!

DON'T FALL OFF THE EDGE OF EARTH!

You're on vacation at the Grand Canyon.
You pull up to a scenic overlook. You scramble out of the car, eager to see the view. But then your mom grabs your elbow, stopping you short. She begs you to be careful. She's afraid you'll fall right over the edge of the cliff!

A long time ago, people had a similar worry about Earth itself. They thought that if they traveled far enough, they might fall right over Earth's edge.

Why would people worry about that? Well, in ancient times, most of the world's great thinkers believed that Earth was flat because it *looked* flat. They could see no obvious clues that they were standing on a round planet.

Scientists in ancient Babylon (modern-day Iraq) believed the universe was made up of six flat layers: three layers of heaven and three layers of Earth. They thought the sky was the lowest heaven, with two heavens above it. Beneath the sky, they said, was the highest level of Earth, where humans lived. They thought that two underworlds, where people went after they died, existed below this layer.

This ancient Greek map shows Earth as a flat disk.

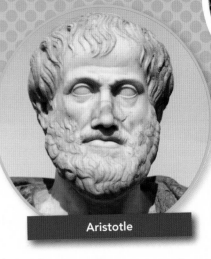

An ancient Greek thinker named Anaximander (610–546 BCE) suggested that Earth was a thick disk with

Aristotle

an ocean in the middle and a ring of mountains surrounding the ocean. In the center of the ocean lay the known world, where humans lived.

The Greek mathematician Pythagoras disagreed. He said that Earth was a sphere, or globe. He believed that the gods would create only a perfect world and that the sphere was the perfect shape. But most Greek scholars still believed Earth was flat.

Around 330 BCE, the Greek scientist Aristotle watched the movements of the sun, the moon, and the stars. He noted that sometimes Earth cast a shadow on the moon and that the shadow was curved. He said the curved shadow meant that Earth was round. Aristotle also pointed out that certain groups of stars appeared high in the sky in southern lands but low in the sky in northern lands. The difference was caused by Earth's round shape, he said.

Aristotle's idea gradually spread. After about 300 BCE, most scientists believed the world was round.

GUMBALL EARTH

Fossil of an ancient reptile

Have you ever bitten into a jumbo gumball? On the outside is a thin, hard candy shell. Under that is a thick layer of gum. And under that . . . nothing. The rest is air, because a gumball is hollow.

Until the 1800s, many people believed Earth was hollow like a gumball. They thought that volcanoes, springs, caves, and wells might be passageways to the hollow interior of Earth. They found fossils, or remains and traces of ancient plants and animals. People thought these strange creatures might have come from Earth's interior. Nearly every ancient culture described an underground world where unusual and powerful beings lived.

British scientist Edmond Halley (1656–1742) thought Earth was mostly hollow. He said that Earth's interior contained three shells, one inside the other, and a lot of empty space. He thought this space was home to living beings and gases. He said that **auroras** were glowing gases that escaped through Earth's **crust** at the poles.

auroras: colored lights that appear in the sky at night, especially in Earth's far north and south

crust: Earth's outermost layer, mostly made of rock

Hot lava flows from a volcano.

Later, scientists learned more about **geology**. They performed experiments on rocks. Scientists also studied magma (melted rock under Earth's surface), lava (melted rock above Earth's surface), and hot springs (groundwater heated by magma). They studied earthquakes and volcanoes. All these studies pointed to the same answer: Earth is not hollow like a gumball. Earth is not even partly hollow.

Earth is packed with solid rock and with liquids such as water and melted rock. It's more like a chocolate-covered cherry. A hard, thin rocky crust lies on the outside. A layer of softer, thicker rock lies beneath the crust. At the core is a solid center, possibly made of iron, surrounded by melted rock. Alas, no strange creatures live deep inside Earth. These exist only in our imaginations.

geology: the study of rocks, mountains, soil, volcanoes, and other physical features of Earth

THE INVISIBLE CONTINENT

You're walking home from school, listening to music through headphones. Suddenly, you feel that someone's behind you. You turn around. You were right! There's a woman about a quarter block back. How did you know she was there? You didn't see or hear her. You just knew.

We sometimes feel very sure about the existence of things we haven't actually seen, heard, felt, smelled, or tasted. This feeling is called intuition. Sometimes our intuition is right. But just as often, it's wrong.

That's what happened with Terra Australis Incognita. This name means "unknown southern land." It was the name for a huge **continent** that people thought covered much of the southern half of Earth. No one had ever seen it, but some scientists were sure it existed.

Ptolemy's map of the world showed a huge southern landmass.

continent: one of seven large landmasses on Earth

Aristotle knew that his neighborhood of Earth, in the northern half of the globe, had a lot of land. He figured that all this northern land was balanced by a lot of land on Earth's southern half. In the 100s CE, the scientist Ptolemy showed this idea in maps. He drew the Indian Ocean as completely surrounded by Africa, India, and another southern land stretching all the way to the South Pole.

In the 1480s, Portuguese explorer Bartolomeu Dias sailed around Africa's southernmost point. This trip showed that Africa didn't extend to the South Pole. In 1520 Ferdinand Magellan, another Portuguese explorer, discovered the same thing about South America.

When European sailors reached Australia in 1606, they believed they'd found Terra Australis. That's how Australia got its name. But in 1642, Dutch explorer Abel Tasman sailed through the Pacific Ocean south of Australia. That trip showed that Australia did not extend to the South Pole.

In the late 1770s, British explorer James Cook sailed all the way around the South Pacific Ocean. He found only ice and some small islands. He didn't get close enough to the South Pole to see whether it was surrounded by land.

In 1820 European sailors spotted mountains on Antarctica. People finally knew that land existed at the South Pole. They also realized the flaws in earlier ideas. Antarctica is a large continent, but it is not the huge southern landmass people long imagined.

James Cook

Early mapmakers drew California as separate from the mainland.

CALIFORNIA DREAMING

You've just heard that a new novel is out. It's bursting with adventure, romance, wizards, giants, and lots of blood. You—and everyone else—can't wait to get your hands on it.

That's how people felt about a book published in 1510. It was *The Adventures of Esplandián* by Garci Rodríguez de Montalvo. The story told of an exciting island called California. According to the book, the island lay close to the coast of North America. It was peopled only by women, overrun with wild animals, and guarded by griffins (imaginary animals that are half lion and half eagle). It was rich with gold too.

Spanish explorers based in New Spain (modern Mexico) set sail on the Pacific Ocean in hopes of finding California. They spotted Baja California. This long, skinny finger of land extended south into the Pacific Ocean. The explorers didn't sail far enough north to see that Baja was attached to North America. They thought it was an island—the California they'd read about. They sent word back to Europe. There, mapmakers drew California as a large island.

Similar maps made the rounds for two centuries. Finally, people exploring by land discovered the sailors' mistake. Between 1698 and 1701, Catholic priests stationed in Baja California traveled north to Tucson, Arizona. Along the way, they noticed the vast wetland where the Colorado River emptied into the Gulf of California. They figured that such a large river drained a very large landmass, something much bigger than an island. The priests described what they'd seen in letters to Europe.

But it took another half century for people to understand that California wasn't an island. Mapmakers continued to show the island of California on their maps.

More explorers traveled through the American Southwest on foot, on horseback, and by boat. Finally, the information they gathered grew too plentiful to ignore. In 1747 King Ferdinand VI of Spain ended the debate with an official proclamation, stating that California was part of mainland North America. At last, Europeans let go of their California dream.

Baja California is a peninsula—a long skinny finger of land. It's attached to the rest of California at the north.

The sun doesn't set at the North Pole in summer, but that doesn't mean it's warm there.

SAILING NORTH TO CHINA

Have you ever heard the expression "dig a hole to China"? In theory, someone could dig all the way through Earth from the Western Hemisphere and surface somewhere in the Eastern Hemisphere (although probably not China). But that's an awful lot of work. And why dig when you could just take a nice sailing trip over the North Pole and then on to China? A few centuries ago, scientists thought that was possible. They believed the North Pole lay in the middle of a warm, open sea.

In the late 1500s, people knew that the North Pole had summers with constant sunlight. That's because the North Pole tilts toward the sun in summer. British scientist William Bourne said that these long summer days warmed up the Arctic Ocean, which surrounds the pole. Also in the 1500s, British explorer John Davis said that all the salt water in the Arctic Ocean kept it from freezing. Other scientists thought that a current of warm water called the Gulf Stream kept waters around the North Pole from freezing.

Businesspeople hoped the scientists and explorers were right. They wanted to ship goods to Asia. Sailing to Asia through the Arctic Ocean would be much shorter and faster than sailing around the tip of South America or Africa.

Sailors in the Arctic often had to cut through the ice to keep their ships moving.

From the 1500s through the 1800s, many expeditions set out to find a sea route through the Arctic. They all failed. Many ships got trapped in the ice. Many sailors died.

In the 1900s, scientists mapped the Arctic using ships, airplanes, and overland expeditions. They found that for most of the year, the Arctic Ocean is completely icebound.

But in summer 2000, scientists noticed that a large area of the Arctic Ocean that was normally covered with ice had become open water. Every summer since, the amount of open water has grown. Scientists think that global climate change is causing this meltdown. If the ice continues to melt, ships might be able to sail north to China after all.

MELTDOWN

Human activities—especially the burning of oil, gas, and coal—add extra carbon dioxide to Earth's atmosphere (the layer of air surrounding the planet). That extra carbon dioxide makes the atmosphere trap more heat from the sun. This process has led to increased temperatures and climate change on Earth.

Have you ever heard someone promise to "move mountains" to achieve something? That means that he or she is going to work like mad to do a very difficult task. "Moving mountains" is just a figure of speech, of course. Mountains can't really move. Or can they?

Until the early 1900s, scientists thought that mountains, continents, and other landforms always stayed put. They thought the continents had always been exactly where they are in modern times.

Early geologists noted that different continents had many connections to one another, however. By examining fossils, scientists saw that the eastern coast of South America and the western coast of Africa once had many of the same plants and animals. On maps, the two continents look like separated pieces of a jigsaw puzzle. Early geologists said that land bridges had once connected the continents. They said these bridges had worn away over time.

Early geologists also said Earth was slowly cooling down and shrinking. They said this shrinkage had caused Earth to "wrinkle," forming mountains.

A German scientist named Alfred Wegener, who worked in the early 1900s, was not satisfied with these ideas. Wegener believed that Earth's continents were once joined into one giant landmass. He said the continents had gradually moved apart over millions of years. He also said

This satellite picture of Earth shows how the continents look like separated puzzle pieces.

that if Earth were shrinking and wrinkling, mountains would be spread evenly around the globe. But they aren't. Wegener thought mountains formed when the edge of one landmass or continent pressed into another, causing the land to crumple.

Wegener couldn't explain what force was strong enough to move continents. So most of the scientific community laughed at him.

Alfred Wegener

But in the end, Wegener was proven right. In the 1960s, scientists began gathering proof of plate tectonics, or the movement of vast **plates** of Earth's crust. These giant pieces hold the oceans and the continents. Scientists learned that plates can crack, move apart, grind against one another, and slide across one another. Over millions of years, the movement of the plates has caused continents to break apart and re-form into different shapes. It has also caused the formation of new seas and mountain ranges. As it turns out, mountains can be moved after all.

plates: about thirty rigid pieces that make up the outer shell of Earth

Two plates rub against each other at the San Andreas Fault in California.

EARTH IS OLD—NO, IT'S YOUNG—NO, IT'S OLD!

When you were little, you probably asked your parents hard questions. Why is the sky blue? Why do puddles disappear? How old is Earth? Scientist have asked the same questions for thousands of years.

Let's look at the question of Earth's age. Aristotle thought Earth had always existed. Others had different ideas. In the first century BCE, the Roman scholar Lucretius studied historical records. Since he couldn't find any history written before the Trojan War, which took place in Greece in about 1200 BCE, he thought Earth was not much older than that. In ancient India, religious scholars said that every 4.32 billion years, the universe exploded, expanded, and then re-formed.

In the Middle Ages (around 500 to 1500 CE), many scholars studied religious texts, such as the Jewish Torah, the Christian Bible, and the Muslim Quran. Based on information in these books, scholars decided Earth was less than ten thousand years old.

Leonardo da Vinci

Then scientists learned more about Earth. In the 1500s, Italian scholar Leonardo da Vinci found seashell fossils in high mountains. This suggested that the mountain peaks had once been underwater. Scientists said that such a big change would have taken much longer than ten thousand years.

This wind-carved rock in Utah shows how layers of sediment build up over time.

In the 1700s, scientists studied erosion, or the wearing away of rock by wind and water. They learned about sedimentation, when tiny particles of sand and rock build up into layers. These studies helped them guess the age of different rock layers.

In the 1800s, William Thomson (better known as Lord Kelvin) studied heat coming from within Earth and heat coming from the sun to Earth. Kelvin guessed that Earth had formed from the sun and had been cooling ever since. He calculated that it had taken between twenty and one hundred million years for Earth to cool to its 1800s temperature. Other scientists guessed ages for Earth ranging from seventy-five thousand to several billion years.

In the early 1900s, scientists studied how certain metals in rock slowly and steadily change form. For example, every 100 million years, about 1.5 percent of a piece of uranium turns into lead. By measuring and comparing the amount of uranium and lead in rocks, scientists could figure out the rocks' age. Using these calculations, they estimated Earth's age to be nearly 4.6 billion years.

In the 1995 movie *Waterworld*, most of Earth is underwater. Life on the liquid planet is very hard. *Waterworld* is set in the future. But the idea of a liquid Earth is an old one. Many religions teach that Earth formed from a vast and deep realm of water.

For about a century, scientists had a similar idea. In 1787 German scientist Abraham Werner put forth a theory called Neptunism. He said that Earth was originally made of water and that the water contained lots of dissolved minerals. Over time, he said, the minerals hardened into **sediment**. These tiny bits of sand and rock piled up into layers of rock. He said the rock built up from Earth's core outward, finally creating all the continents. Werner called the lowest, oldest, and hardest rock layers primitive rocks. He called the next layers transition rocks, followed by secondary rocks and finally loose rocks on top.

Around the same time, Scottish geologist James Hutton devised a theory called Plutonism. He said that all

Abraham Werner

sediment: small particles that settle to the bottom of bodies of water

Earth's rocks had formed by the slow cooling of melted minerals. He argued that some rocks formed inside Earth when magma cooled. He said other rocks formed when lava flowed from volcanoes and then cooled. He also said that heat and pressure deep inside Earth caused rocks to change form.

James Hutton

In 1820 Italian engineer Giuseppe Marzari-Pencati studied some rock layers near Predazzo, Italy. He found granite (an example of Werner's "primitive rock") lying over white marble (one of Werner's "secondary rocks"). According to Neptunism, this was impossible, since primitive rock was supposed to be the innermost layer.

WHAT'S IN A NAME?

Neptunism was named after Neptune, the ancient Roman god of the sea. Plutonism got its name from Pluto, the ancient Roman god of the underworld.

More geologists studied the rocks at Predazzo. By the late 1800s, most geologists agreed that processes deep inside Earth had formed these rocks. They believed the same forces formed rocks worldwide. Plutonism had won the day.

Modern geologists list three types of rocks. Igneous rocks form from cooled lava or magma. Sedimentary rocks form from hardened layers of sediment. Metamorphic rocks are those that change form inside Earth. For example, heat and pressure deep underground can turn limestone into marble. Marble is an example of a metamorphic rock.

LET'S MAKE SOME GOLD!

Got a hankering for gold but no money to buy some? No problem—at least not if you're living in Europe in the Middle Ages. Your city or town might be home to a scientist called an alchemist. Alchemists believe that gold can be made from less valuable metals. If you can be just a *little* patient, your friendly neighborhood alchemist promises, he'll soon have the proper gold-making formula.

While you're waiting for your gold, let's talk about the history and practice of alchemy. Alchemy began as the study of different metals and other substances. Alchemists believed that if they could mix substances together properly, they could help people live longer—perhaps even forever. This study developed separately in several ancient societies, including ancient Egypt, India, and China.

In the ancient Middle East, alchemists thought that all metals, including gold, were made up of mercury and sulfur in different amounts. European alchemists liked this idea.

A painting from the 1600s shows a European alchemist at work.

They wanted to figure out the proper formula for making gold from mercury and sulfur. They also borrowed an idea from Chinese alchemists. They said that to make gold from less valuable metals, you needed an object called the Philosopher's Stone. This stone would not only help create gold but would also grant eternal life.

Sound a little silly? It didn't in the Middle Ages. In fact, governments took alchemy very seriously. At one time, the government of England outlawed alchemy, hoping to prevent people from making gold and gaining too much wealth and power.

Alchemists never did find the Philosopher's Stone. Nor did they find the formula for creating gold from other metals, or the secret for eternal life.

But alchemy did contribute lots of knowledge to the scientific world. Alchemists combined different substances and examined how different substances reacted with one another. These experimenters were the first chemists. One famous alchemist-turned-chemist was Irishman Robert Boyle. In the 1600s, Boyle searched for ways to turn other metals into gold. He never succeeded, but his experiments formed the basis for modern chemistry and physics.

Robert Boyle

Settlers in 1888 plow the cornfield surrounding their sod home in Nebraska.

RAIN FOLLOWS THE PLOW

It's 1883. You're a young adult ready to strike out on your own as a farmer. You've heard exciting things about the Great Plains, a vast land between the Mississippi River and the Rocky Mountains. Folks used to call it the Great American Desert, but no more. You hear that ever since farmers started settling there in the 1870s, the desert has turned green. Folks say that rainfall is plentiful there. They say, "Rain follows the plow."

In the 1870s, this wasn't just a folk saying. It came straight from scientists. They said that farmers coming to the Great Plains made the climate wetter. They said trains stirred up the atmosphere and increased rainfall. They also explained that newly planted trees and crops added oxygen and water vapor to the air, creating more rain. They said that breaking up the soil with plows allowed soil to soak up more rainwater. This too added moisture to the air, the scientists said.

An enormous cloud of dust, known as a dust storm, darkens the sky over Oklahoma in 1935.

In the 1880s, rain on the Great Plains was plentiful. Crops grew well. Rain dwindled in the 1890s, but it returned in the new century. For the next three decades, rain fell faithfully.

In 1931 the rain stopped again. This time, the **drought** was longer and more severe. Without rain, crops wouldn't grow. Without crops, there were no plant roots to hold the dry dirt in place. Wind blew dirt from farmers' fields. Giant dust storms rolled over the Great Plains. The drought and dust destroyed farms. People grew poor and hungry.

Scientists had thought that people settling the Great Plains had caused its plentiful rain in the 1870s and the 1880s. But when twentieth-century scientists looked at long-term weather records, they realized that the Great Plains has a normal cycle of rain and drought. In the late 1800s, settlement and rain happened at the same time purely by chance.

Modern farmers know how to better protect the soil so it won't dry out and blow away. Plowing along the curves of the land instead of in straight lines keeps soil in place. Planting trees and shrubs between fields helps break the wind and capture rainwater.

drought: a long period with little or no rain

BUNDLE UP—WE'RE HEADED FOR ANOTHER ICE AGE!

Have you been living alone in a cave, with no contact with the outside world? No? Then you probably know that Earth is slowly warming up. You know that this warming is causing climate changes all over the planet. You're learning about it in school, seeing it in the news, and maybe even having severe weather where you live.

Scientists suspected global warming long ago. Some spotted signs, such as melting glaciers (giant bodies of ice), as far back as the early 1800s. Temperatures on Earth gradually grew warmer from the mid-1800s to the 1940s. In the mid-1900s, scientists said that global warming was really happening—and that humans were causing it. They explained how burning oil, coal, and gas added extra carbon dioxide to the air, trapping heat from the sun.

But people were slow to be convinced. That was partly because from the 1940s to the early 1970s, Earth started cooling off. Temperatures dropped during this period.

Scientists quickly figured out that air pollution was causing this cooling. Pollution from cars and factories

A chunk of ice breaks off Monaco Glacier in Norway. Warming global temperatures are causing large bodies of ice to melt.

contains tiny particles called aerosols. These particles block sunlight. Volcanic eruptions also blast aerosols high into the air. For a few decades, aerosols from pollution and volcanoes acted like a shade. They reduced the amount of sunlight reaching the ground. This shading worked against global warming.

In the 1970s, a few scientists wrote that cooling caused by aerosols might bring about a new **ice age**. The news media ran amok with this idea. In June 1974, *Time* magazine published an article titled "Another Ice Age?" The idea of global cooling spread far and wide.

Many scientists were skeptical, however. They didn't think the cooling would lead to a new ice age. What is more, the cooling trend ended shortly after it was spotted. In the 1970s, many governments passed stricter pollution laws. This helped reduce aerosol levels. Volcanoes also erupted less often. As a result, global warming started up again.

Over the last 2.6 million years, Earth has had several ice ages, separated by warmer periods. Scientists say that if humans weren't pouring so much carbon dioxide into the air, the next ice age would hit within two thousand years. But humans continue to add carbon dioxide to the air. So we probably won't be bundling up for an ice age anytime soon.

ice age: a period in Earth's history when ice sheets covered vast areas of land

Do you like to explore the great outdoors? Do you go camping or hiking in remote places? If so, you'd better keep your eyes peeled. A dinosaur could be lurking in some swamp. A woolly mammoth might be around the next corner. And let's hope you don't bump into a saber-toothed tiger!

Wait a minute, you say. Those animals are all **extinct**. They died out thousands or millions of years ago. People have found fossil remains of the creatures, but no one's ever seen them alive.

If you had made this argument in ancient times, you would've angered some famous scientists. The idea of extinction flies in the face of an ancient scientific principle: the *scala naturae* (ladder of nature). According to this theory, simpler life-forms are on the bottom of the ladder and more complex life-forms are on top. Aristotle believed in the *scala naturae*. Up until the 1700s, many European scientists believed it too.

Europeans called this idea the Great Chain of Being. They said extinction was impossible. If a species (a type of animal or plant) died out, they said, the chain would break and life

extinct: no longer existing. An animal or plant becomes extinct when every one of its kind has died.

on Earth would fall into chaos.

A few scientists disagreed. In the 1790s, a French naturalist named Georges Cuvier carefully studied elephant fossils found near Paris, France. He noted that their bones were quite different from bones of living elephants in Africa and India. They were also

This illustration from 1579 shows the Great Chain of Being.

different from bones of elephant fossils found in Siberia. Cuvier declared that the bones came from a separate elephant species that had gone extinct.

Cuvier's argument was convincing. Clearly, there were no ancient elephants still walking around on Earth. If there were, someone would have seen them. By the mid-1800s, most scientists accepted that many ancient plant and animal species had become extinct.

So the next time you go exploring, watch for bears, alligators, or wolves. But don't worry about saber-toothed tigers. They're gone for good.

Georges Cuvier

FURTHER INFORMATION

The Dynamic Earth
http://www.mnh.si.edu/earth/main_frames.html
The Smithsonian Institution's interactive site teaches about Earth science. It includes sections on gems and minerals, rocks and mining, plate tectonics and volcanoes, and the solar system.

Earth Observatory
http://earthobservatory.nasa.gov
On this website, join scientists from the National Aeronautics and Space Administration as they explore our world and unravel the mysteries of climate and environmental change.

Exploratorium
http://www.exploratorium.edu
At this website, a project of the Exploratorium science museum in San Francisco, California, you'll find lots of information, activities, videos, and apps that will help you learn about—and have fun with—a wide variety of science topics, including geology and ecology.

Geology for Kids
http://www.kidsgeo.com/geology-for-kids
This website offers an in-depth online geology textbook written for kids. Learn about the world beneath you, how it formed, and how it changes.

Geology of the United States
http://nationalatlas.gov/geology.html
This US government-sponsored website provides detailed information about the terrain of the United States.

Ice Stories: Dispatches from Polar Scientists
http://icestories.exploratorium.edu/dispatches
Visitors to this website can read about the thoughts and experiences of scientists working in Antarctica and the Arctic.

Margles, Samantha. *Mythbusters Science Fair Book.* New York: Scholastic, 2011. This book is packed with dozens of myth-busting science fair projects you can do at school or at home.

Storad, Conrad J. *Uncovering Earth's Crust.* Minneapolis: Lerner Publications, 2013.
The outside layer of our planet is an active place. Earth's crust is always changing. You can learn all about it in this interesting book.

Strange Science
http://science.discovery.com/strange-science
At this Science Channel website, you can explore science hoaxes, science feuds, science mistakes, and more. In addition to a treasure trove of fascinating information and photographs, this website includes many videos, kids' activities, and interactive features.

TIME. *TIME Nature's Wonders: The Science and Splendor of Earth's Most Fascinating Places.* Minneapolis: Twenty-First Century Books, 2009.
This book presents a portrait of planet Earth, with information on oceans, geology, the atmosphere, and climate.

Walker, Sally M. *Figuring Out Fossils.* Minneapolis: Lerner Publications, 2013.
Studying ancient plants and animals tells us more about our own existence. Have you ever searched for fossils? You'll unearth some in this book.

YES!. Hoaxed! Fakes and Mistakes in the World of Science. Tonawanda, NY: Kids Can Press, 2009.
This book uncovers and explains seventeen brilliantly bogus stories from the history of science.

INDEX

PHOTO ACKNOWLEDGMENTS

The images in this book are used with the permission of: © javarman/Shutterstock.com, p. 2, 5 (top left), 10 (top), 11 (top); © James Steidl/Shutterstock.com, p. 4; © Sergey Skleznev/Dreamstime.com, p. 5 (top right); © R. Gino Santa Maria/Shutterstock.com, p. 5 (bottom); NASA/GSFC/NOAA/USGS, p. 6 (top); © English School (19th Century)/Private Collection/The Bridgeman Art Library, p. 6 (bottom); NASA/GSFC/NOAA/USGS, p. 7 (bottom); Jastrow (2006)/Ludovisi Collection/Wikimedia Commons, public domain, p. 7 (top left); NASA/GSFC/NOAA/USGS, p. 7 (top right); © De Agostini Picture Library/De Agostini/Getty Images, p. 8; © Juliengrondin/Dreamstime.com, p. 9; © North Wind Picture Archives/Alamy, p. 10 (bottom left); © frantisekhojdysz/Shutterstock.com, p. 10 (bottom right); © Museum of New Zealand Te Papa Tongarewa/Gift of New Zealand Government, 1960 /The Bridgeman Art Library, p. 11 (bottom); Library of Congress/Wikimedia Commons, pp. 12 (top), 13 (top); © Steve Collender/Shutterstock.com, p. 12 (bottom); © Caroline Warren/Digital Vision/Getty Images, p. 13; © Elisa Locci/Alamy, p. 14 (left); © David W. Leindecker/Shutterstock.com, p. 14 (right); © BThaiMan/Shutterstock.com, p. 15 (bottom); © The Stapleton Collection/The Bridgeman Art Library, p. 15 (top); © iStock/Thinkstock, p. 16 (bottom right); © Todd Strand/Independent Picture Service, pp. 16 (top), (bottom left), 17 (middle); © SZ Photo/Knorr+Hirth/DIZ Muenchen GmbH, Sueddeutsche Zeitung Photo/Alamy, p. 17 (top); © Lloyd Cluff/CORBIS, p. 17 (bottom); © Stock Montage/Archive Photos/Getty Images, pp. 18 (main), 29 (bottom left); © Xpixel/Shutterstock.com, p. 18 (19 rocks); © David Davis/Taxi/Getty Images, p. 19 (main); © Bianchetti/Leemage/The Bridgeman Art Library, p. 20 (bottom); © 117 Imagery/Flickr Open/Getty Images, pp. 20 (top right), 21 (bottom left); © Ilizia/Shutterstock.com, p. 20 (top left), 21 (bottom left); © Christie's Images/The Bridgeman Art Library, pp. 21 (top), 22; © Fitzwilliam Museum, University of Cambridge, UK/The Bridgeman Art Library, pp. 22 (top), 23 (middle); World History Archiver/Newscom, p. 23 (bottom right); © I. Pilon/Shutterstock.com, pp. 23 (bottom left), 23 (top); The Granger Collection, New York, pp. 24, 25; © Yamada Taro/Digital Vision/Getty Images, p. 24 (25); © Sebastian/Alamy, p. 26 (bottom); © Kichigin/Shutterstock.com, p. 26 (27 snowflakes); © Eduard Harkonen/Shutterstock.com, p. 26 (27 icicles); © Image Source/Getty Images, p. 27 (top); © Tim Bewer/Lonely Planet/Getty Images, pp. 28, 29 (bottom right); © David Herraez Calzada/Shutterstock.com, p. 29 (top left); © The Italian School, (16th century)/Private Collection/The Bridgeman Art Library, p. 29 (top right). Front cover: © Moneymaker11/Shutterstock.com (gold coins); © Vitaly Korovin/Shutterstock.com (gold nuggets).